21ST-CENTURY ECONOMICS

UNDERSTANDING SUPPLY AND DEMAND

ERICA OWOEYE

Cavendish
Square

New York

MIDLOTHIAN PUBLIC LIBRARY
14701 S. KENTON AVENUE
MIDLOTHIAN, IL 60445

Library of Congress Cataloging-in-Publication Data

Names: Owoeye, Erica, author.
Title: Understanding supply and demand / Erica Owoeye.
Description: New York : Cavendish Square, [2020] |
Series: 21st-century economics | Audience: Grades 7-12. |
Includes bibliographical references and index.
Identifiers: LCCN 2018057078 (print) | LCCN 2018057439 (ebook) |
ISBN 9781502646101 (ebook) | ISBN 9781502646095 (library bound) |
ISBN 9781502646088 (pbk.)
Subjects: LCSH: Supply and demand--Juvenile literature. |
Economics--Juvenile literature.
Classification: LCC HB801 (ebook) | LCC HB801 .O96 2020 (print) |
DDC 338.5/21--dc23
LC record available at https://lccn.loc.gov/2018057078

Editorial Director: David McNamara
Editor: Chet'la Sebree
Copy Editor: Nathan Heidelberger
Associate Art Director: Alan Sliwinski
Designer: Joe Parenteau
Production Coordinator: Karol Szymczuk
Photo Research: J8 Media

The photographs in this book are used by permission and through the courtesy of: Cover image,
Robert Cicchetti/Shutterstock.com; cover background and repeated throughout the book, Champ008/
Shutterstock.com; p. 4 iQoncept/Shutterstock.com; p. 7 Andrey Popov/Shutterstock.com; p. 9 Giannis
Papanikos/Shutterstock.com; p. 10 Andy Dean Photography/Shutterstock.com; p. 15 Hurst Photo/
Shutterstock.com; p. 17 SilverStar/File: Supply-demand-right-shiftsupply/Wikimedia Commons/GNU
Free license, CCA 2.5 Generic; p. 18 Eviart/Shutterstock.com; p. 20 Benoit Daoust/Shutterstock.com;
p. 26 James Steuart/BEIC Digital Library/File: Steuart, Inquiry into the principles of political oeconomy,
1767 - 5727474.tif/Public Domain; p. 31 Hulton Archive/Getty Images; p. 33 The Denver Post/Getty
Images; p. 34 David Nance, ARS/USDA/File: Feld mit reifer Baumwolle.jpeg/Wikimedia Commons/
Public Domain; p. 37 Stock Montage/Getty Images; p. 40 Ryan McVay/Photodisc/Getty Images; p. 42
Africa Studio/Shutterstock.com; p. 44 Dotted Yeti/Shutterstock.com; p. 48 Digitaler Lumpensammler/
Moment/Getty Images; p. 50 NickEyes/Shutterstock.com; p. 53 Ekrub-ntyh/File: Oil producing
countries map.png/Wikimedia Commons/CCA-SA 3.0 Unported; p. 55 Jeff Schmaltz, MODIS Rapid
Response Team, NASA/GSFC/http://visibleearth.nasa.gov/view_rec.php?id=7938/File: Hurricane
Katrina August 28 2005 NASA.jpg/Public Domain; p. 56 Steve Byland/Shutterstock.com; p. 60
Vlastas/Shutterstock.com; p. 63 Perutskyi Petro/Shutterstock.com; p. 66 Chesky/Shutterstock.com.

Printed in the United States of America

CONTENTS

GOODS AND SERVICES

The wealth and resources of a country or region, especially in terms of the creation and usage of goods and services, make up its economy. Economics is a social science that focuses on how people use their limited resources. It is the study of the production, distribution, consumption, and transfer of wealth in society. The law of supply and demand is one of the most important principles of economics.

The Law of Supply and Demand

Supply and demand represent the amount of goods and services available in comparison to the amount of goods and services people want to purchase. The law of supply and demand is a main factor in determining the price of

Opposite: Supply and demand work together. Several factors go into bringing the two into balance.

goods and services. If a product is in high demand and a manufacturer has a limited supply, the company can charge more for it. People will be willing to pay a high price to get their hands on the item. Similarly, if demand for a product is low, then the manufacturer may have to lower its prices to lure customers.

When we think of supply and demand, we often think of products we can purchase, like electronics, food, or clothing. A manufacturer decides how much of its product to make based on the demand of consumers. The creator of the product might also base supply decisions on how he wants his product or brand to be perceived. For instance, if he wants the item to be exclusive or considered a luxury item, he may only make a small quantity. This way, he can sell his limited product for a higher price.

Similarly, a service provider focuses on the efficiency and availability of its service. Its prices change depending on the demand of consumers. If there are four nail salons in a tiny town, each salon will have to keep its prices low to be competitive. Since there is a high supply of the service, the individual providers need to do their best to attract customers.

Different Types of Goods and Services

There are many different ways that goods and services are affected by supply and demand. For instance, club goods are affected by supply and demand. Club goods are those that many people can use at once but that some can be excluded from using. This exclusion can be because of capacity. For instance, only a certain amount of people can fit in an amusement park. People might be excluded from the park simply because it has reached the maximum amount of people allowed in the park that day. With

Loyalty cards can provide discounts. However, sometimes a company decides customers can't use specific benefits. Often, these decisions are the result of supply and demand.

these club goods, a discount is usually offered to attract customers at times when demand is expected to be low. However, there may be periods of time when customers aren't allowed to use these discounts because the demand is expected to be high. So, for instance, an amusement park may offer discounts during the winter months to attract customers. However, in the summer, people cannot use these discounts because the amusement park owners know there will be more than enough people who will come during the warmer months.

Similarly, common goods are another type of good affected by supply and demand. Water is an example of a common good. Although it may not seem like it, common goods still have a limited supply. These goods are in high demand, and their common use leads to their depletion. In order to protect their supply, changes must be made to adjust the way they are used. Often, government agencies like the Environmental Protection Agency (EPA) are involved in managing the supply and demand of common goods through laws.

Supply and demand also affect assets, or valuables that people own, such as real estate. Demand for these assets can increase or decrease sharply based on a variety of factors, including people's incomes. People's incomes are affected by the job market. When a specific set of skills is desired by businesses, the amount they are willing to pay for those skills will go up. This drives up the supply of these skills as people work to acquire them to earn higher salaries. As people have higher salaries, they are more willing to spend money on big-ticket items such as homes.

We will dive deeper into some of these examples of supply and demand in the first chapter.

On Black Friday and days on which popular products are released, crowds of people line up to be the first to purchase the products. These crowds reflect an increase in demand.

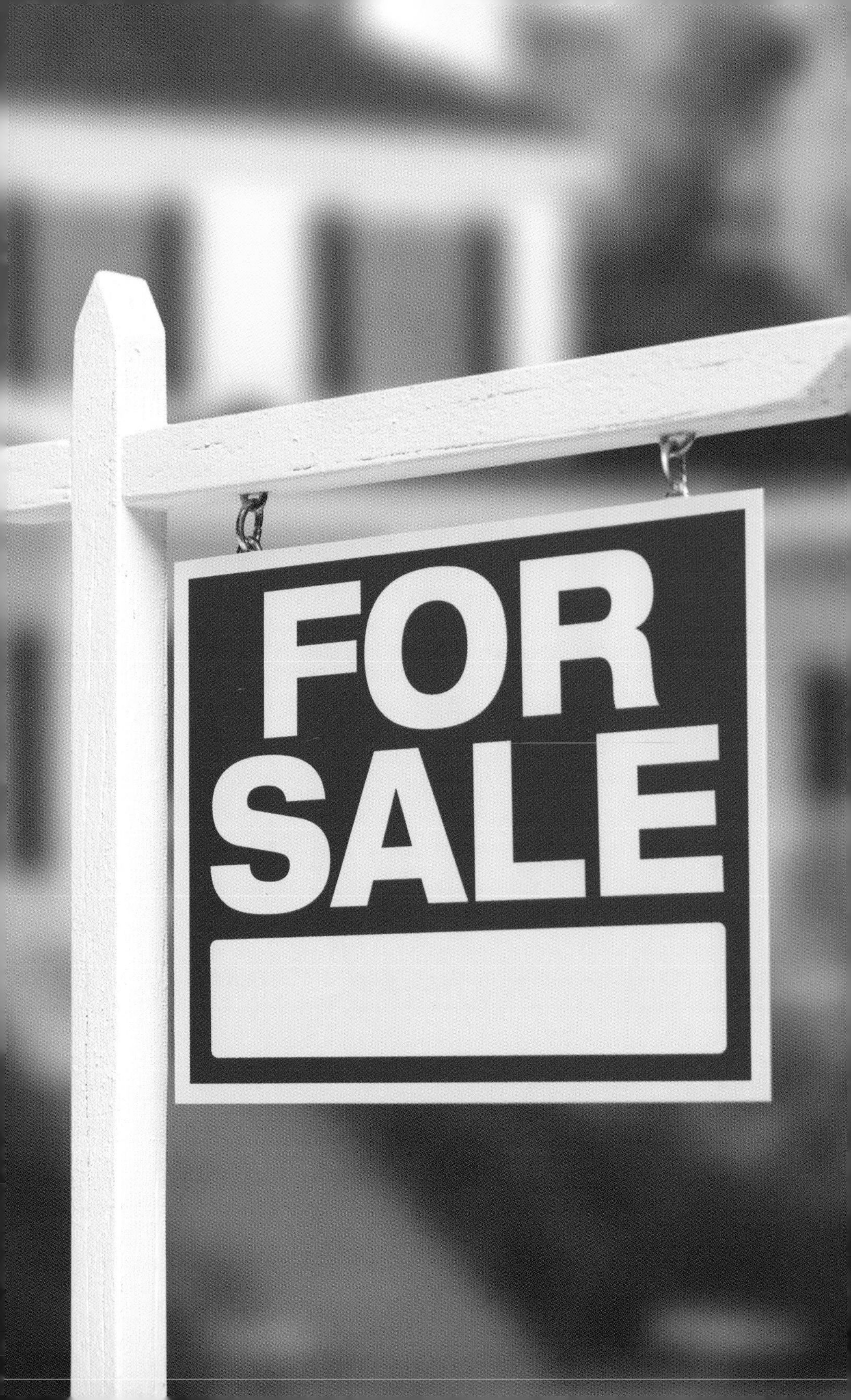
FOR
SALE

CHAPTER 1

DEFINING SUPPLY AND DEMAND

Supply refers to how much of something the market can offer. It is the quantity of a good or service available at a specified price. A number of influences can determine supply. Similarly, a number of factors go into determining the demand for a good or service. Demand refers to how much of something buyers want or are willing to purchase.

Determining Supply

Supply of a good or service is determined by price, the cost of inputs or labor, the number of competitors, and producers' expectations. Price has a major effect on supply. For a company, the higher the price of a good or service, the more profitable it is. The more profitable it is, the

Opposite: Most things for sale or purchase are affected by the law of supply and demand, from food and haircuts to cars and houses.

more the producer will make or provide. A manufacturer makes more of a good, increasing supply, in hopes of selling more. However, it is important for suppliers to be cautious of the price. If a price is too high, then people won't buy the good or service.

The costs related to making a good or service also affect its supply, as they also determine the profits a supplier or provider can make. If the parts that go into making a good or the costs of the labor of those making the good are low, then it is easier to produce a lot of it in order to make a profit. The opposite is also true. High costs to provide the good or service will decrease supply as a manufacturer or provider is trying to keep costs low.

Technology also affects the costs of inputs or labor. Often, technology and new machinery allow manufacturers to produce goods more quickly and at a lower cost. Technological advances can also make a manufacturer's current process obsolete, or out of date. Outdated machinery can slow down a supplier's ability to produce a good in comparison to others in the same market. For instance, imagine Coca-Cola has a new machine for making plastic bottles that cuts production time in half. This increases Coca-Cola's supply so much that the company can sell more of their product at a lower price. This will tempt people to buy more Coca-Cola.

Pepsi, in order to stay competitive, may need to invest in similar machinery.

That brings us to our fourth influence on supply: competition. More competition generally means less supply. As more producers enter a market, it affects how much each producer is willing or able to sell. For instance, perhaps there was only one coffee shop in a small town in 2010. That one shop would supply the town with most of its coffee. By 2015, however, there were four coffee shops in a four-block radius. The number of people living in the area has remained the same. That means that each coffee shop may have to supply less because they are all trying to provide the same number of people with coffee.

Similarly, a producer's expectations can affect supply. If a manufacturer notices that a competitor may have a similar product coming out, it may increase its current supply. In that way, the original manufacturer can sell more of its product before there is competition. These expectations may also affect the cost of production, especially if producers are rushing to manufacture items. Additionally, these expectations may affect the price of the good.

As you can see, the elements that go into determining supply are fairly interconnected, or linked. Demand, however, also plays a critical role.

Determining Demand

Economists recognize five factors that influence demand. The first is income. As people's incomes increase, their ability and willingness to purchase goods and services at a given price will also increase. This willingness to spend money then causes an increase in demand for goods and services. The opposite occurs after a decrease in people's incomes or a rise in unemployment.

Another factor in determining demand is marginal utility. This has to do with the amount of satisfaction or usefulness gained from a good or service lessening after each additional purchase of it. For example, you purchased a copy of Harper Lee's *To Kill a Mockingbird* for class. It is unlikely that you'll purchase another unless you lose your copy or purchase it as a gift for someone else. Purchasing two copies from the start, however, does not increase the book's usefulness or your satisfaction. In this way, the product's low marginal utility affects demand, as it is likely you'll only purchase the amount that's useful to you. Manufacturers and producers take this into account when considering the demand for their products.

Substitution goods also affect demand. Substitution goods are goods that cater to the same need. For instance, Sprite, Sierra Mist, and 7UP could be considered substitution goods. All three are caffeine-free, lemon-lime-flavored sodas. However, they are all produced by different companies. A change in price by one company affects the demand for the others. For instance, if a six-pack of Sprite is two dollars while six-packs of Sierra Mist and 7UP are three dollars, then the demand for Sprite is likely to increase. At the same time, the demand for Sierra Mist and 7UP will likely decrease.

Complementary goods work in a similar way. Complementary goods are products that go together, like peanut butter and jelly. Demand for one is connected to the demand for the other. If the price for one increases, then it is likely that the demand for both will decrease.

Two different products that can drive a change in the supply and demand of each other, like peanut butter and jelly, are called complementary goods.

Finally, demand is influenced by consumers' changing tastes. Changes in fashion styles, for instance, result in increased demand for some products and decreased demands for others. For instance, flared jeans were popular in the early 2000s, whereas skinny jeans were more popular in the 2010s. The demand for certain styles changed, and jean manufacturers had to respond to keep up with the changing times.

Supply and Demand Curves

Supply and demand work together based on the amount of a good or service available and the amount of that good or service customers desire, creating a market for the product. The two can be depicted graphically as the supply curve and the demand curve.

The supply curve shows the quantity of a good or service supplied at different price levels. Price is represented by the y-axis. The quantity supplied is represented by the x-axis. The supply curve normally slopes upward, reflecting the need for a higher price to cover the increased production costs that come with producing more goods.

The demand curve shows the quantities of a good or service a consumer would be willing to buy at various prices. The axes are the same as those used to represent the supply curve. The demand curve generally slopes

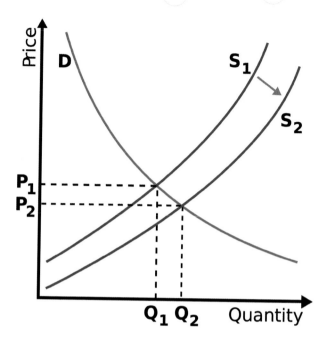

When the cost to manufacture a product decreases, the quantity produced will increase, causing the supply curve (*shown in blue*) to shift to the right.

downward. This reflects that the higher the price, the lower the demand will be for the good or service.

Reaching Equilibrium

Where these two curves intersect, or where supply equals demand, is the market equilibrium. The market takes place any time potential sellers of a good or service meet with potential buyers to exchange money for said good or service. Equilibrium can be defined as a balance. Any

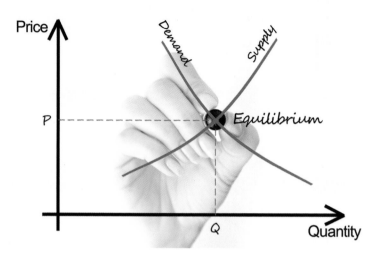

Price

Demand

Supply

P ----------------------- Equilibrium

Q

Quantity

When the supply and demand curves meet, the right balance of price and quantity produced have been achieved, resulting in market equilibrium.

time opposing influences are balanced, an equilibrium is reached. What causes this balance between supply and demand? The key is the price.

If consumers look to buy more of a product than is available at the current price, the price tends to go up. As the price rises, the quantity offered usually increases as well. However, the willingness of consumers to pay the higher price often decreases when this happens. If consumers want to buy less of a product, the price tends to go down. The measure of the responsiveness of supply and demand to the changes in price is called price elasticity. Once consumers are satisfied with the price and willing to purchase the product, and manufacturers are able to produce the good for profit at that price, supply and demand are balanced. Market equilibrium is reached.

Examples of Supply and Demand

In what other ways can we illustrate changes in supply and demand? Let's look at examples in a few different categories of supply and demand. A producer has to decide how much of a product to make available to consumers. The company may decide to make less of the product to keep the brand considered a luxury. For example, a producer of a luxury handbag may only make, or supply, five thousand handbags in a specific style. If the company sold this handbag at $1,000 per bag, the demand would be limited, as few consumers would be willing or able to purchase a handbag at this high price. The limited demand means that the company could probably sell out of the product in a year. Supply and demand would be equal, while the company maintains its luxury status.

If the company sold this handbag for $100 per bag, however, the demand would be much higher, as more people would be able to afford it. Higher demand would mean the company would likely produce more of its product, particularly to cover the costs of production. This increased availability and affordability, however, may affect the company's brand. It may no longer be seen as a luxury company. That is something certain companies consider.

Managing Demands on Services

Another example of supply and demand surrounds service providers. A service provider focuses on being efficient

Increasing subway ticket prices during rush hour times can help to encourage riders to shift their schedules to avoid these higher rates. This change helps reduce demand and congestion.

while keeping the price affordable for its customers. How might a public transportation system, such as the New York City subway, be more efficient without increasing the number of trains, which would increase the cost of providing the service?

In 1952, William Vickrey proposed a new pricing system for the NYC subway. He recommended increasing fares during peak travel times and in areas with high traffic. The peak travel times were morning and afternoon rush hours during the work week. He also recommended that fares be lowered at all other times and in low traffic areas. This is known as "congestion pricing." These fares would encourage commuters with more flexible hours to travel during non-peak times. The resulting spread of passenger traffic over time would reduce pressure on the system and allow an even larger total passenger count.

Managing Common Goods

Air, more specifically clean air, is in demand by all of us. We need it to survive. However, clean air is limited, with all of the pollution from cars and manufacturing companies. This high demand and limited supply of clean air makes it a common good. The demand for air is not likely to go down, so what can be done to increase the supply or at least slow down the depletion of air that is safe to breathe?

The United States Environmental Protection Agency, also known as the EPA, has put regulations in place that mandate specific processes that polluters must use to meet emissions standards. This means that there is a limited amount of pollution that they can produce. Taxes and fees may be charged for pollution emissions over a certain level. These taxes and fees encourage companies to find ways to reduce pollution to save money. Some products, specifically some pesticides, have even been banned by the EPA in an attempt to save our supply of air.

Managing Assets

Real estate is an asset that has a fixed supply. Even though the United States, for instance, is fairly large, more land isn't necessarily being created. Of course, things can occur to make small increases in the supply. For instance, high-rise buildings can be built to fit a lot of living space on a small piece of land. Similarly, a large piece of land can be divided into smaller lots where individual homes can be built and then sold.

The demand for real estate, however, can go up and down drastically. One reason for this is interest rates. An interest rate is the amount a bank can charge someone who takes out a loan. For instance, a 10 percent interest rate on a $200,000 loan means that a borrower will owe the bank at least $220,000 when paying back the money.

If interest rates on mortgages, or home loans, decrease, then more home buyers are likely to enter the market. This increased demand for real estate will cause house prices to go up. This will, in turn, decrease the demand as potential home buyers back off, waiting for prices to go back down to buy.

The Job Market

Something that can create changes in supply and demand is the job market. Consumers must have a source of income in order to have the money needed to demand the products, services, and assets mentioned above. Meanwhile, the job market itself has its own law of supply and demand to follow.

A change in technology can cause a change in the types of job skills employers need or want. In other words, the demand for employees has changed. For instance, an employer may be in search of software engineers with knowledge of Ruby, a programming language. The employer will offer an increased salary for engineers with knowledge of it. The increase in salary drives people to learn to program using Ruby. As a result, there will be an increase in the supply of Ruby developers in the job market. A new Ruby developer now has the income to buy the house she has been considering.

THE ROLE OF GOVERNMENT

The US government regulates supply and demand through the use of monetary and fiscal policies. Monetary policy gives the Federal Reserve, the central bank of the United States, the power to raise or lower interest rates. The interest rates that banks are allowed to offer make it easier or harder for individuals to borrow money. In theory, when money is more expensive to borrow, demand for goods goes down. As demand decreases, the hope is that so will the prices of goods and services.

Fiscal policy is the government's power of spending and taxation. During a recession, or a period of significant decline in spending activity across the economy, the government may increase its spending and decrease taxes to give money back to businesses and consumers. This encourages more buying and selling. During a time of inflation, when prices are rising and the value of money is falling, the government may increase taxes to reduce consumers' spending and drive prices down.

A government can also set price floors and ceilings. These limits set the minimum or maximum price for which a specific good can be sold. An example of this is rent control. It institutes a maximum price that landlords can charge tenants.

An example of how other government regulations can affect supply and demand can be seen when the government calls for new safety laws for cars, like air bags or emissions controls. When this happens, the cost of car production goes up to meet these standards. The car manufacturers have to make up this cost somewhere, which often results in charging more to the consumer and supplying fewer cars.

A N

INQUIRY

INTO THE

PRINCIPLES OF POLITICAL OECONOMY:

BEING AN

ESSAY ON THE SCIENCE

OF

Domeſtic Policy in Free Nations.

IN WHICH ARE PARTICULARLY CONSIDERED

POPULATION, AGRICULTURE, TRADE, INDUSTRY,
MONEY, COIN, INTEREST, CIRCULATION, BANKS,
EXCHANGE, PUBLIC CREDIT, AND TAXES.

By Sir JAMES STEUART, Bart.

Ore trahit quodcumque poteſt atque addit acervo. HOR. Lib. I. Sat. I.

IN TWO VOLUMES.

VOL. I.

LONDON:
Printed for A. MILLAR, and T. CADELL, in the Strand.
MDCCLXVII.

CHAPTER 2

THE HISTORY AND DEVELOPMENT OF SUPPLY AND DEMAND

Where did the idea of supply and demand get its start? The principle behind the law of supply and demand was recognized well before it was given its name. There were several British philosophers and economists responsible for the early discussion of this economic concept.

Opposite: Sir James Steuart first used the words "supply and demand" in his 1767 work *Inquiry into the Principles of Political Economy.*

Early Economists

John Locke was an English philosopher and physician. He was born in 1632 in a small village in southwestern England. Locke was a student at the University of Oxford and held a number of positions there after completing his degree.

In his 1691 publication, *Some Considerations of the Consequence of the Lowering of Interest, and Raising the Value of Money*, Locke discusses the law of supply and demand. It is discussed in connection with interest rates in seventeenth-century England. Merchants, or suppliers, wanted the government to lower the amount private lenders could charge people who wanted to borrow money. This is an example of monetary policy.

Locke disagreed with the push for this policy. He felt the prices should be set by the free market, or the supply and demand of goods and the competition between businesses, rather than by the government. Locke believed interest rates would regulate themselves based on "the proportion of buyers and sellers." In other words, he believed that the market would balance itself naturally. Although he never used the phrase "supply and demand," he helped provide an explanation of the concept that James Steuart would name over seventy-five years later.

The economic usage of the words "supply and demand" first appeared in print in 1767 in Steuart's

Inquiry into the Principles of Political Economy. Steuart, born in Scotland in 1712, attended the University of Edinburgh. In his 1767 book, he considers the effects of supply and demand on workers. Steuart recognized that when supply is higher than demand, prices had to be lowered to sell the goods. As a result, merchants made less of a profit and could no longer afford to pay their workers. This resulted in high unemployment.

Economics Guided by Supply and Demand

Adam Smith, a philosopher and an economist, is best known for his 1776 work entitled *The Wealth of Nations*. In this book, he builds on Steuart's term "supply and demand." He describes a scenario where everyone is satisfied by an economy that is guided by supply and demand. This is the concept of laissez-faire. The term, French for "allow to do," is a philosophy or practice in which the government is minimally involved in economic matters. Smith, like Locke, agreed with a more hands-off approach. His work went on to inspire others like David Ricardo.

Born in London in 1772, Ricardo began working with his father, a successful stockbroker, at the age of fourteen. A stockbroker is someone who helps people buy and sell stocks. Ricardo worked as a stockbroker and loan broker and became interested in economics after reading Smith's *The Wealth of Nations*.

After taking up economics, Ricardo wrote *Essay on the Influence of a Low Price of Corn on the Profits of Stock* in 1815. In this essay, he argues that repealing, or getting rid of, the Corn Laws would provide more wealth to productive members of society. The Corn Laws were trade restrictions on imported food and grain, including corn, in Great Britain between 1815 and 1846.

The law imposed a high tax on imported grains. This tax made it too expensive to buy grains from other countries. It remained high even when the local supply was low. This allowed British landowners to charge high prices for grain because it was the only supply to which the British had access. Ricardo believed in free trade, a policy that allows goods to be imported and exported between countries without restrictions. In response, Ricardo wrote about why countries should participate in international trade even when they are capable of producing a good themselves.

Economists on Equilibrium

In 1877, Léon Walras, a French economist, published *Elements of Pure Economics*. In this work, Walras describes the main principles of general equilibrium theory. He explains the theory of supply, demand, and prices in an

In the nineteenth century, people formed clubs and collected signatures to protest the Corn Laws. The laws drove up food prices in Great Britain by placing a high tax on imported grain.

economy with multiple interacting markets. This theory attempts to prove that the interaction of supply and demand will result in an overall equilibrium. Walras built a system to show that price and quantity are determined separately for each good. He was greatly influenced by Antoine-Augustin Cournot, a former schoolmate of his father.

Cournot was a French economist and mathematician born in 1801. He focused on partial market equilibrium. He believed the market was controlled by merchants whose only goal was to maximize profits. He ignored the idea that the customer must also benefit from the exchange to continue to call for a product.

Cournot was the first to draw a demand curve to show the relationship between price and the demand for a good. He showed that the most profitable amount of a good to produce is the amount where the marginal cost, or the extra amount of money needed to produce one more unit of a good, is equal to the marginal revenue, or the extra money earned from selling that one additional unit. Marginal revenue can also be defined as the gross revenue, or the amount of profits after expenses, generated from the last unit sold. These ideas were actually forgotten until they were discovered again by Joan Robinson years later.

An Early Female Economist

Robinson was born in England in 1903. She earned a degree in economics from the University of Cambridge

Joan Robinson, a professor at the University of Cambridge, was one of the only female economists of her time.

COTTON TAKES THE THRONE

Although there were many conversations surrounding economic theories in the nineteenth century, the realities of supply and demand could be seen in the markets. During the first half of the nineteenth century, cotton production was booming in the southern part of the United States. Since cotton was produced by enslaved laborers, production costs were low. This meant that the price of cotton was relatively low. This low price enabled fabric makers to expand production and keep the prices of

Following the Civil War and the abolishment of slavery in 1865, the production of cotton decreased significantly.

their products low. It meant that cotton was marketable and was making plantation owners quite wealthy.

Additionally, cotton accounted for more than half of the value of all exports out of the United States by the mid-1830s. The economic boost from the export of cotton resulted in the expansion of other manufacturing and the need for food and other goods in cities throughout the United States, creating other markets. It's no wonder James Hammond, an attorney, politician, and planter from South Carolina, said in 1859, "Cotton is king!"

Following the Civil War and the emancipation of slaves in 1865, however, the production of cotton decreased significantly. The end of slavery resulted in a labor shortage, as there was no longer the manpower to pick the cotton. This resulted in a decrease in the supply of cotton.

Former slaveholders, no longer able to afford to keep up their land, were forced to break up plantations and rent out portions. This, along with the large amount of money spent on the war itself, led to severe poverty in the South. People could no longer afford to buy the goods made from cotton. This resulted in a decrease in the demand. Cotton no longer stimulated the economy. Cotton was no longer king.

in 1925 and taught at the university from 1931 to 1971. Robinson became a full professor of economics in 1965. She discussed competition and monopolies in her first major book, *The Economics of Imperfect Competition*, published in 1933. A monopoly is when a single company has the exclusive control of the supply of a particular good or service. For instance, if McDonald's purchased all other fast-food companies and converted them into McDonald's restaurants, the company would have a fast-food monopoly.

In addition to her important work on competition and monopolies, Robinson also challenged supply and demand theories and models. Primarily, she questioned their usefulness in predicting the future. She also wondered how they accounted for the past.

The Development of Today's Theories

Alfred Marshall, born in London in 1842, was a skilled mathematician and economist. He compiled many of the aforementioned theories to develop them into modern economic concepts. For instance, his *Principles of Economics*, published in 1890, developed the supply and demand curves that continue to be used to illustrate the point of market equilibrium.

Alfred Marshall was a mathematician and economist whose theories of supply, demand, and market equilibrium are the concepts we use today.

Marshall also introduced a concept that studied how prices affect demand. This is the idea of price elasticity. It was generally understood that an increased price stops people from buying a product, or lowers the demand. However, Marshall felt this was not true all the time. Some products, like food or medications, remain in demand regardless of price. He called these goods inelastic to describe how a price increase does not decrease the demand because the good is viewed as necessary by consumers.

Marshall also noted that competitors are aware of what others are doing. They will set prices accordingly to avoid selling too low or paying too high of a price for labor. The consumers within the market behave similarly. They pay attention to what others are paying for the same goods or services.

Marshall also explored the equilibrium of supply and demand. He noted that if the demand price is greater than the supply price, then sellers will receive more than enough profit to continue to bring the good to the market to meet the demand. This extra money enables the company to increase their rate of production, which would hopefully increase their profits if the demand price remains sustainable. However, when the demand price is less than the supply price, the seller is not making enough of a profit to continue to bring the good to the market. In that case, the seller will most likely stop producing the good. When the demand price and the supply price are equal to one another, the seller will continue to produce the item at the same pace. There is no reason to increase or decrease the rate of production. Equilibrium has been reached. Marshall believed this equilibrium was the point where both buyers and sellers could be satisfied.

CHAPTER 3

A MARKET IN DISEQUILIBRIUM

A market may not always find equilibrium. A disequilibrium, or lack of stability, can occur due to a number of factors. Some of these factors include social pressures, government regulations, and inelastic prices. A market in disequilibrium can lead to a surplus of a supply, or a supply greater than the demand. It can also lead to a shortage of a supply, or a supply that is too little to meet the demand. In some cases, adjustments will be made to achieve market equilibrium.

A Social Contract

A business may intentionally keep it prices low out of a feeling of obligation to its community or loyal customers.

Opposite: The United States government sets a minimum price, or price floor, on milk to allow farmers to continue to earn a profit regardless of changes in supply and demand.

The company makes this decision for a social reason. For example, a landlord named Jesse is currently charging $1,500 per month to rent each of his apartments. Usually, landlords increase the rent each year. This year, Jesse chooses to keep the rent increases low on his properties. He only charges an additional $50 per month each year his tenants sign a new lease. He does this even though his neighboring landlords are charging $2,000 per month.

While he could make more by charging $2,000 per month, Jesse knows several of his current tenants cannot afford it. Raising the monthly rent by $500 a month would cause the tenants to find another apartment. It would likely mean that these individuals would have to find another community altogether, since other landlords in

If the supply of apartments is low and demand for apartments is high, landlords might raise rent prices because interested tenants might be willing to pay more.

the area are already charging $2,000 per month. Jesse does not want to see this happen. He grew up in this community and knows many of his tenants personally. He does not want to see them forced to relocate. He already earns a profit, so he continues to keep annual increases as low as possible.

As a result, he has zero turnover in his properties. This results in a shortage of apartments available to those looking to move into the neighborhood. This causes a disequilibrium. It can be fixed, however. Property developers can build new apartment buildings or buy properties to rent out to increase the supply to meet the demand. Equilibrium might also be reached if Jesse is forced to sell his property.

Floors and Ceilings

Sometimes there are the minimum and maximum prices that the government allows businesses to charge for some products. The government might set a price floor if a product is important to the economy but companies are struggling to make enough money selling it. To be effective, the price floor must be set above the equilibrium, the price where supply meets demand. For instance, the government sets a minimum on the price of a gallon of milk. The equilibrium price is two dollars per gallon. This is the price consumers are willing to pay and the price that

When supply and demand are not in balance, the market is in disequilibrium. This often results in businesses losing money.

allows suppliers to meet their demand. The equilibrium price is too low, however, for the dairy farmers to make a profit. To help these dairy farmers earn a profit, the government sets the price floor of a gallon of milk at three dollars. Because of this higher price, there may, at times, be a surplus of milk as consumers lower their demand for the product. This causes a disequilibrium. However, the higher price of milk is generally reasonable enough that people will continue to purchase milk, providing the famers with a profit.

Inelastic Prices

Sticky or inelastic prices are prices that remain the same, or are slow to react, when there are changes in the supply or demand of a good or service. Restaurants often have sticky prices. Imagine a restaurant paying to print new menus every time there is a price change to the goods they purchase. It would get quite expensive. It makes sense for the restaurant to keep their prices sticky for a period of time, not always changing to match the market equilibrium and not always following the law of supply and demand.

Similarly, a product that relies on another product does not necessarily change its price every time the price changes on the needed product. For instance, the price of spaghetti sauce does not go up or down as frequently as, or in response to, the price of tomatoes. Imagine the price of tomatoes has gone up due to a shortage of the tomato crop this year. As a result, the spaghetti sauce brand is paying more to produce its sauce. Although the law of supply and demand tells us the price of spaghetti sauce should go up, the price remains the same. The price of sauce is sticky. When there is a strong crop of tomatoes and the price drops to sell off the surplus, the spaghetti sauce price does not go down. The brand simply enjoys higher profits during that time.

QUICK Q&A

How does an increase in minimum wage affect supply and demand?

An increase in minimum wage may cause prices of goods to go up as a direct result of the increased cost of labor. Prices may also go up because of the increase in demand for goods by consumers who are now earning higher wages.

How does the change in seasons affect demand?

One season ending and another beginning can make a difference in the types of goods and services in demand by consumers. The end of summer means the end of fresh local fruit and vegetables in some areas of the country. Having to buy strawberries grown in California, at a higher price, will reduce the amount of strawberries in demand in South Dakota. This will likely cause grocery stores to reduce the amount of strawberries they supply. Similarly, the change in seasons changes the demand for the types of clothing consumers want to buy. As a result, the supply shifts as well.

Although some goods and services have sticky prices, others are subject to ups and downs as they try to reach market equilibrium.

The Avocado Market

Consumption of avocados in the United States has tripled since the year 2000. It seems you can get them on everything, from salads to burgers. Do you want a few slices of avocado added to your club sandwich? Do you want guacamole on your burrito bowl? That will cost extra. Although the price you pay for added avocado at a restaurant might stay sticky, the price you pay for an avocado at the grocery store is subject to change.

What factors come into play in setting that price? For avocados, the crop can greatly vary from one year to the next. One reason for this is that avocados grow on an alternate bearing cycle. This means that one year a tree will bear, or produce, a large crop. The next year, it will produce less. Then, the following year, it will bear more again.

Avocados grow in places like Southern California, Florida, Puerto Rico, Mexico, Australia, and New Zealand because they require a climate with little wind, plenty of water, and minimal frost to survive. A drought or a frost will result in a shortage of avocados for a period of time. This shortage will cause the price of avocados to be higher. The demand will remain high until, eventually, the amount of consumers willing to pay the higher price will lower to reach equilibrium. In the reverse, a high-bearing year in conjunction with the right weather will result in a surplus of avocados. This high quantity of avocados will cause the price to fall. Demand will go back up, and again, market equilibrium will be reached.

If you live in one of these regions where avocados are grown, you are likely eating locally grown avocados. You likely pay a lower price because of this. Someone in Pennsylvania, however, is eating avocados shipped from somewhere like California or Florida. That person pays a higher price than someone living in Southern California

Avocado crops can vary greatly from year to year. These increases and decreases in the supply affect the price of avocados at the grocery store.

when purchasing avocados from the grocery store because the grocery store had to pay for the shipping.

The demand for avocados in the United States alone is so great that the supply cannot possibly be met by just the crops grown in the few avocado-producing regions within the country. Overall, the greatest percentage of avocados sold in the United States comes from Mexico. In fact, Mexico is the largest international exporter of avocados worldwide.

What would happen to prices of avocados if the United States and other countries imposed a border or import tax on all goods coming from Mexico? This tax is paid by the exporter of the avocados. To balance out the tax, these farms or companies will likely charge a higher price to those companies that want to import the avocados. It is likely, then, that the importers will increase the price they charge avocado consumers to make up at least a portion of the new cost of doing business. In this case, the price increases not because of a shortage in crops but because of the increased cost involved in getting the supply to the consumers.

Demand was originally high, but will it stay high given this new price? Or will the demand be reduced, leaving the avocado producers with a surplus? Will the market find equilibrium? All of these answers depend on consumers' spending habits.

CHAPTER 4

THE EFFECTS OF SUPPLY AND DEMAND ON OIL

Crude oil is a fossil fuel. This type of fuel forms through natural processes, such as the decomposition of dead organisms. It exists as a liquid underground and within spaces of sedimentary rocks, such as sandstone or shale. Oil reserves exist all over the world, but the countries that produced the largest supplies in 2017 were the United States, Saudi Arabia, Russia, Canada, and China. Once the crude oil is removed from the ground, it is separated into petroleum products, such as gasoline, diesel fuel, heating oil, jet fuel, and asphalt. The five countries in the world that used the largest amount of these products in 2016 were the United States, China, India, Japan, and Russia. In

Opposite: Offshore platforms, such as the one shown here, drill for crude oil located beneath the seabed.

the United States, petroleum is the largest source of energy. It is used to run vehicles, to heat homes and buildings, and to generate electricity.

Oil Prices

The law of supply and demand determines the price of crude oil and the prices of the products created with the oil. Prices influence the behaviors of consumers, eventually shifting the amount of demand for oil. In turn, this affects the supply and pricing. For example, a long period of high gasoline prices will make consumers look for ways to use less gas and save money. People might switch to using public transportation or buy a vehicle that is more fuel-efficient. As a result, demand for oil will go down.

The Organization of the Petroleum Exporting Countries

What other factors can cause changes in oil prices? The Organization of the Petroleum Exporting Countries, or OPEC, plays a large part in determining oil prices. OPEC is an alliance of fifteen countries: Algeria, Angola, Ecuador, Equatorial Guinea, Gabon, Iran, Iraq, Kuwait, Libya, Nigeria, Qatar, the Republic of the Congo, Saudi Arabia, the United Arab Emirates, and Venezuela. These fifteen countries produce around 40 percent of the world's oil

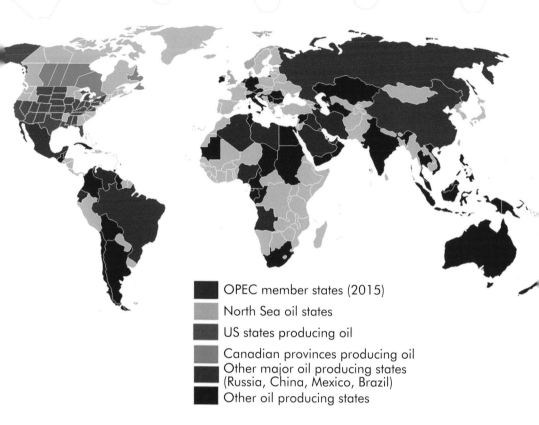

OPEC member states (2015)

North Sea oil states

US states producing oil

Canadian provinces producing oil
Other major oil producing states
(Russia, China, Mexico, Brazil)
Other oil producing states

The Organization of the Petroleum Exporting Countries, or OPEC, plays a large part in determining oil prices. However, there are many oil-producing countries around the world.

supply. They determine the amount of production based on the global demand. They influence the price of oil by increasing or decreasing production. For example, in mid-2014 oil prices lowered dramatically after OPEC refused to reduce oil production.

This price drop had a major effect on Venezuela in particular. Oil accounts for over 90 percent of

Venezuela's exports. The country's economy suffered from the low prices. In the midst of a financial crisis which caused high inflation rates, the oil production in the country decreased dramatically. For instance, in 2017, the country produced 2 million barrels of oil per day. By September 2018, the country was only producing 1.4 million barrels per day.

Politics

Political unrest can cause price fluctuations in oil as well. The summer of 2018 saw the highest gasoline prices in four years. What caused this price hike? A few factors. The possibility of oil supply disruptions in Libya and Nigeria spooked the markets. Both countries faced important political elections that could have resulted in the end of a civil conflict and a major change in power, respectively. Global investment companies worried about the political unrest, as they thought fighting and riots could cause a loss of half a million oil barrels per day from the two countries combined. Similarly, missile strikes against Syria, missile attacks targeting oil-producing cities in Saudi Arabia, and fears of a trade war affected the price of oil.

Because oil prices are set in a globally integrated market, these issues increase prices worldwide, regardless of where the actual supply of oil is coming from. For example, the United States produces around 80 percent

Natural disasters, such as hurricanes, can have a large impact on oil prices as well as the supply of goods like water.

of its oil supply but will still feel the effects at the pump when other oil-producing countries are experiencing a decreased supply.

Natural Disasters

Natural disasters also have a major influence on oil prices. In the United States, oil rigs located in the Gulf of Mexico just offshore from Texas, Louisiana, Mississippi, and

A NEW START

Let's consider how a factory relocating can shift supply and demand in both the original and new cities. In this example, a chair manufacturer is the main employer for those living in a community. Changes in technology and necessary increases in the cost of labor cause the company to look for ways to reduce costs. It makes the decision to invest in a new technology that will allow the company

When a business closes up shop in one location, it causes a shift in the supply and demand for the goods and services it provided in its local community and business sector.

to employ fewer workers and to move the factory to a city with a lower cost of living. Therefore, the chair manufacturer can pay lower wages to fewer employees. This reduction in costs will enable the company to keep prices low. This allows it to compete with other furniture companies, while increasing its overall profits.

In the city where the factory is closing its doors, the former employees are now forced to look for new jobs. This increases the demand for jobs. The loss of income causes a decrease in demand for other goods and services in the area. People may move from the city in search of work, increasing the supply of housing.

In the city where the chair company moves, jobs are created, increasing the supply of jobs. The increase in jobs increases income. The increase in income results in an increased demand for other goods and services, as consumers are now more willing and able to buy them. Employees from the factory's prior location may have been offered the opportunity to relocate to the new location. As a result, there can be an increased demand for housing.

Alabama make up a major oil-producing region. When Hurricane Katrina hit that area in 2005, 19 percent of the United States oil supply was affected. The destruction caused a reduction of supply, while demand remained the same. The result affected the entire country. Within days of the hurricane, there were gas shortages in South Carolina, the Dakotas, Arkansas, and Kentucky. In other places, prices quickly surged.

Natural disasters can also cause roads to be blocked and power outages for several days or weeks. When this happens, fuel companies have difficulties making shipments. This drastically lowers the supply in some areas, causing the types of shortages mentioned above. Gas stations are forced to increase prices in an attempt to keep their businesses in operation until the next shipment can arrive. Since merchants tend to sell their goods at the prices consumers are willing to pay, some businesses increase prices after a natural disaster simply because people are desperate. This practice is known as price gouging. This happens when prices are higher than what most would consider reasonable or fair.

Oil as Energy

Although we've primarily discussed how gas prices affect drivers, it is important to note that oil prices affect people who don't drive at all. Often, oil is used to generate electricity, and most people in the United States use electricity in their homes. This means that the changing oil prices affect people's electricity bills.

There are a few different technologies used to transform oil into electricity. One way is the use of steam. Oil is burned to heat water to create steam to turn a turbine, a wheel or rotor whose motion generates electricity. Burning oil, however, produces a great amount of air pollution. In addition to high oil prices driving up the cost of electricity use, the pollution created when converting oil to electricity can cause consumers to look for difference sources of power.

Changing Behaviors

When the price of crude oil goes up, consumers end up paying more at the pump to run their vehicles. They pay more in utility bills to heat their homes and use electricity. As these prices continue to increase, consumers will begin looking for other ways to get what they need. Environmental concerns also cause consumers to look for ways to reduce their carbon footprint, or emissions given off from the use of fossil fuels. This can cause an increase in demand for alternative sources of energy.

CHAPTER 5

DEMANDING ALTERNATIVE ENERGY

Rapidly growing economies around the world have the opportunity to build with energy efficiency and environmental friendliness in mind. This mindset can reduce long-term costs as well as protect the environment from further harm. Businesses, specifically utility companies, that invest in energy efficiency programs can see a number of benefits. For one, they can avoid the increased costs associated with emissions, such as the taxes and penalties some countries have put in place on emissions over a certain level. The demand for alternative energy, increased efficiency, and increased environmental friendliness can also cause job growth.

Opposite: Oil- and coal-burning power plants generate electricity while producing substantial air pollution. However, there are alternatives, like the nuclear plant in this picture.

Job Growth and Cross-Elasticity

Imagine a company establishes a contract with an energy service company to install its technology to conserve energy. The energy service company needs to hire more workers to keep up with the continued increase in demand for these types of technologies. Indirectly, the company that manufactures the parts to create the energy-saving devices also has to hire more workers to supply enough of its product to meet the increased demand. The newly employed workers spend their new income on goods and services in their local economies, further promoting more job growth in the area. The individuals that are now experiencing lower energy bills also spend their savings on other goods, like clothing. Economists refer to this as cross-elasticity. This happens when the reduction in the price of one good or service causes increased demand for another good. For our example, falling energy costs result in increased retail sales.

Alternative Energy: Wind

One alternative source of power is wind energy. Wind energy makes use of a renewable source, or a resource that can be used repeatedly and is replaced naturally. Like other alternative energy sources, wind energy does not generate any waste. The wind is used to spin a generator—a machine that converts energy into electricity.

Wind turbines and solar panels are alternate sources of energy. They reduce the reliance on oil, while also generating little to no waste.

Most states within the United States have some wind turbines and continue to invest in the technology. In 2017, there were nearly sixty thousand wind turbines across the country. This energy-efficient technology, however, is quite expensive to install. As we've learned, though, an increased interest by consumers increases the demand and can drive down price. If more areas invest in wind power, the technology will become more affordable.

There are, however, some very real limitations to wind power. Some areas are prone to lower wind speeds. For instance, parts of Tennessee have some of the lowest average wind speeds in the country. This means that the technology wouldn't be particularly useful in those areas. Demand isn't likely to increase, which means that the technology won't necessarily get cheaper in Tennessee.

Alternative Energy: Solar

Another alternative source of electricity, and one individuals can use for their homes, is solar power. This source is completely renewable, and the money saved on traditional utility bills far outweighs the cost of installation of solar panels in the long run. However, people need the money for the solar panels up front as opposed to stretching payments out over time through utility bills.

Some countries have programs in place to encourage the use of solar panels. The United States, for example, has a Solar Investment Tax Credit. This credit allows individuals and businesses to deduct a portion of the cost of installing solar panels from their taxable income. This reduces the total amount of federal taxes owed. When weighing the cost of solar energy against traditional energy sources, a tax credit like this can be enough to inspire consumers to choose solar. Even still, demand for renewable solar technology remains fairly low because people don't always have the money for the actual installation.

Conserving Energy

Besides changing the source of the energy being used, consumers can also find ways to conserve energy by simply using less. The price of the utilities may remain high, but consumers can reduce demand by reducing the amount they need or use. What are some ways that this can be done?

There are a number of ways for consumers to conserve energy. One way is to install energy-efficient technologies and appliances in their homes. In the United States, tax credits may be offered for taking steps like purchasing energy-efficient appliances and windows. Heat gain and loss through windows accounts for about 25 percent of heating and cooling energy use. Windows that have double panes and a frame made of material to help reduce heat transfer can help save energy costs. Similarly, consumers can also change driving habits to use less gasoline. They can both reduce the amount of gasoline they have to purchase and the amount of carbon emissions put into the air. They may trade in a gas-guzzling vehicle for a more fuel-efficient one.

In the twenty-first century, hybrid cars have become popular. Hybrids use a combination of a standard engine that requires gasoline and a battery-operated electric system to increase fuel efficiency and reduce emissions.

Consumers can change the type of cars produced by suppliers by increasing demand for cars that use less gasoline and emit less pollution into the air.

A FEW MORE FACTS

- A supply curve is a graph that represents the relationship between the price of a good and the quantity of the good the producer is able to supply. A change in the cost to produce the good will cause a shift in the curve. Less of the good will be able to be produced if the cost increases.

- A demand curve is a graph that represents the relationship between the price of a good and the amount of it that consumers are willing and able to purchase. A change in the public's interest in a good will cause a shift in the demand curve. As demand increases or decreases, and the price that consumers are willing to pay adjusts accordingly.

- Market equilibrium occurs when the quantity demanded and the quantity supplied are equal. This is where the supply and demand curves intersect.

- Price elasticity is a measure to show the responsiveness of the price of a good or service when there are changes in the supply or demand of the good or service. Remember, some prices are sticky and cannot respond as quickly to the changes in supply and demand.

- Some factors that influence supply and demand are price, income levels, consumer tastes and preferences, fashion, change in seasons, and competition.

When the car accelerates, both the gasoline engine and the electric motor work together to increase the car's power. As previously discussed, car makers have also been tasked with lowering car emissions. As a result of the increased demand for more fuel-efficient vehicles and the increased costs of making them, the prices for cars go up to allow the car manufacturers to have the funds to increase supply to the necessary levels to meet the demand.

Additionally, an increase in the price of oil and oil-related products causes consumers to find other means of reducing the amount of money they are spending on items that they cannot live without. Since hybrid and battery-operated cars are expensive, they are not the answer for everyone. Some people may be better served by using public transportation to commute to and from work. This way they can spend their money elsewhere. As more people rely on public transportation, the demand for oil and cars will decrease. Meanwhile, the demand for books may increase as people purchase more books to read while they're riding public transportation.

The End Game

With any good or service, market equilibrium is the goal. This is tricky with oil because of the world's constantly changing political landscape, weather, and needs. In fact, in general, market equilibrium can be difficult to achieve because supply and demand are constantly changing based on everything from unemployment rates to fashion seasons. For these reasons, prices, jobs, and the overall economy will ebb and flow in response to the changing needs of people and countries.

GLOSSARY

alternative energy A source of power that avoids using fossil fuels.

carbon footprint The amount of carbon dioxide emitted due to the use of fossil fuels.

consumer An individual who buys a good for his or her personal use.

cross-elasticity The responsiveness of the quantity demanded of one good or service when the price of another changes.

demand The need or want of a good or service.

disequilibrium A loss or lack of stability in the balance of supply and demand.

economist An expert in the knowledge of the production, consumption, and transfer of wealth.

elasticity The measure of how much the price of a good or service can change in response to changes to its supply or demand.

emissions Pollutants produced and released into the air.

equilibrium The state in which opposing influences are balanced, like when supply meets demand.

fossil fuels Fuels like oil formed over a very long period of time by natural processes, such as the decomposition of dead organisms.

inflation An increase in prices and/or a decrease in the value of money.

marginal cost The extra cost added when one additional unit of a good or service is produced.

market The arena in which buyers and sellers affect supply and demand through the exchange of goods and services.

monopoly The exclusive control of the supply of a particular good by a single company.

price gouging When a seller increases the price of a good to a level that is much higher than is considered reasonable or fair.

recession A period of time when trade and industrial activity are low, which causes a slowdown in economic growth.

supply The amount of something that is needed or wanted.

FURTHER INFORMATION

Books

Frazer, Coral Celeste. *Economic Inequality: The American Dream Under Siege*. Minneapolis: Twenty-First Century Books, 2018.

Kishtainy, Niall. *The Economics Book: Big Ideas Simply Explained*. London, UK: DK, 2012.

Small, Cathleen. *Wind, Waves, and the Sun: The Rise of Alternative Energy*. The History of Conservation: Preserving Our Planet. New York: Cavendish Square, 2018.

Weeks, Marcus. *Heads Up Money*. London, UK: DK Children, 2017.

Websites

Econlowdown.org

https://www.econlowdown.org/supply-and-demand?module_uid=120&p=yes

This site uses interactive graphs to show changes in supply and demand and prices.

Renewable Energy World

https://www.renewableenergyworld.com

Renewable Energy World provides news, information, and resources about renewable energy.

Videos

Demand and Supply—EconMovies #4: Indiana Jones

https://www.youtube.com/watch?v=RP0j3Lnlazs

This video gives examples of supply and demand using scenes from *Indiana Jones and the Temple of Doom*.

Ford Is Scrambling to Limit the Impact of Stopping F-Series Production

https://www.cnbc.com/video/2018/05/09/ford-is-scrambling-to-limit-the-impact-of-stopping-f-series-production.html

This video explains the supply and demand issues Ford faced after a fire at a plant halted production.

Organizations

Department of Finance Canada
90 Elgin Street
Ottawa, ON K1A 0G5
Canada
(613) 369-3710
Website: http://www.fin.gc.ca

The Department of Finance Canada ensures a healthy Canadian economy by developing sound economic policies and providing expert advice to the government.

Economic Development Administration

US Department of Commerce
1401 Constitution Avenue NW, Suite 71014
Washington, DC 20230
Website: https://www.eda.gov
(202) 482-5081

The Economic Development Administration is an agency in the US Department of Commerce that stimulates commercial and industrial growth while also providing grants and assistance to generate new jobs.

Environmental Integrity Project

1000 Vermont Avenue NW, Suite 1100
Washington, DC 20005
(202) 296-8800
Website: https://www.environmentalintegrity.org

The Environmental Integrity Project is a nonprofit organization that advocates for more effective enforcement of environmental laws. Two former EPA attorneys founded the organization in 2002.

Environment and Climate Change Canada

Fontaine Building, 12th Floor
200 Sacré-Coeur Boulevard
Gatineau, QC K1A 0H3
Canada
(819) 938-3860
Website: https://www.canada.ca/en/environment-climate-change.html

Environment and Climate Change Canada informs Canadians about protecting and conserving their natural heritage, in addition to promoting and ensuring a safe and sustainable environment.

United States Agency for International Development

Ronald Reagan Building
1300 Pennsylvania Avenue NW
Washington, DC 20004
(202) 712-0000
Website: https://www.usaid.gov

This independent US government agency provides foreign aid and development assistance.

United States Environmental Protection Agency

1200 Pennsylvania Avenue NW
Washington, DC 20460
(202) 564-4700
Website: https://www.epa.gov

The EPA is an independent US government agency responsible for the protection and conservation of natural resources as well as human health.

SELECTED BIBLIOGRAPHY

Bannock, Graham, and R. E. Baxter. *The Penguin Dictionary of Economics*. 8th ed. New York: The Penguin Group, 2011.

"Economic and Employment Impacts of Energy Efficiency." United States Agency for International Development, October 1, 2018. https://www.usaid.gov/energy/efficiency/economic-impacts.

"Economic Incentives." United States Environmental Protection Agency, February 1, 2018. https://www.epa.gov/environmental-economics/economic-incentives.

"Electricity from Oil." Power Scorecard. Accessed October 1, 2018. http://www.powerscorecard.org/tech_detail.cfm?resource_id=8.

"Frequently Asked Questions." US Energy Information Administration. Accessed December 12, 2018. https://www.eia.gov/tools/faqs.

"How Does the Law of Supply and Demand Affect the Oil Industry?" Investopedia, August 24, 2018. https://www.investopedia.com/ask/answers/040915/how-does-law-supply-and-demand-affect-oil-industry.asp.

Lioudis, Nick K. "What Causes Oil Prices to Fluctuate?" Investopedia, April 20, 2018. https://www.investopedia.com/ask/answers/012715/what-causes-oil-prices-fluctuate.asp.

"Oil: Crude and Petroleum Products Explained." United States Energy Information Administration. Accessed September 28, 2018. https://www.eia.gov/ energyexplained/index.php?page=oil_use.

Patton, Mike. "The Facts on Increasing the Minimum Wage." *Forbes*, November 26, 2014. https://www. forbes.com/sites/mikepatton/2014/11/26/the-facts- on-the-minimum-wage-increase/#4fc789f133a1.

Rodrik, Dani. *Economics Rules: The Rights and Wrongs of the Dismal Science*. New York: W.W. Norton & Company, Inc., 2015.

Schwartz, Elaine. "The Mystery of the Disappearing Avocado." *Econlife*, May 7, 2017. https://econlife. com/2017/05/rising-avocado-prices.

Spacey, John. "9 Examples of Supply and Demand." Simplicable, January 2, 2018. https://simplicable. com/new/supply-and-demand.

"Supply and Demand Introduction." Shmoop. Accessed September 10, 2018. https://www.shmoop.com/ supply-demand.

Taylor, B. "Price Floors." Fundamental Finance. Accessed September 25, 2018. http://economics. fundamentalfinance.com/micro_price-floor.php.

"Who Discovered the Law of Supply and Demand?" Investopedia, August 31, 2018. https://www. investopedia.com/ask/answers/030415/who- discovered-law-supply-and-demand.asp.

INDEX

ABOUT THE AUTHOR

Erica Owoeye has been an accountant, with a focus on payroll, for fifteen years. She grew up in and lived in a small city in northwestern Pennsylvania until she relocated to the Washington, DC, area in 2008. She has always had an interest in mathematics and finance, loving when she sees that the figures on a balance sheet are accurate. Additionally, she's invested in learning how things work and how processes can be improved.